Modern Graphics Programming Primer

Hans de Ruiter

Rev 1.4 – 2023 – Added SDL_HINT_OPENGL_ES_DRIVER to OpenGL (ES 3.x) init code
Rev 1.3 – 2019 – Reformatted for print
Rev 1.2 – 2019 – Reformatted for e-book readers
First Edition, 2017

Share the Link
Know someone who would benefit from this book? Give them the following link so they can get their own copy:
https://keasigmadelta.com/graphics-primer

Table of Contents

Introduction

Congratulations on deciding to read this primer! It's been written to accompany an OpenGL tutorial series called "Getting Started with OpenGL ES 3+ Programming" (which you can get from this link https://keasigmadelta.com/gles3-sdl2-tutorial-amz). I'm sure your ultimate goal is to create visually impressive games and apps, and the tutorial series will teach you what you need to get started.

So, why this book then? Well, understanding how a Graphics Processing Unit (GPU) works and the theory they're built on will make you a more effective graphics programmer. Think about it for a moment, if you understood *how* a machine works, *what* it can do and *why*, would you be better at using that machine. Absolutely!

This book will give you this extra knowledge. Once you understand how the GPU works you'll be able to think creatively instead of blindly following tutorials. You'll think of better ways to achieve the results you want, and possibly even come up with new techniques.

Let's not get ahead of ourselves, though. We need to learn the fundamentals first, and that's what this primer delivers. It'll be as light on mathematics as possible, focusing on concepts instead. This book's goal is *accelerated learning*. I want you to get up to speed as quickly as possible, and have included the key concepts needed for you to achieve this.

This book is best read together with the tutorial series (see https://keasigmadelta.com/gles3-sdl2-tutorial-amz if you don't have the tutorials). That way you'll alternate between learning the theory and putting it into practise. The tutorials periodically refer to relevant sections in this book.

Reading this book by itself is fine too, though.

Overview of the Modern GPU

Modern GPUs (Graphics Processing Units) are a type of processor that's optimized for rendering graphics. They typically have thousands of processing cores that can process vast quantities of data in parallel.

There's a catch though, the cores can't execute totally different code like a CPU's core can. Instead, they all run a handful of programs known as *shaders*. That restriction is fine for graphics, though, because we're performing the same operations on thousands to millions of vertices and pixels at a time.

Mythbusters Adam Savage and Jamie Hyneman demonstrate this principle using robots in this entertaining video: https://youtu.be/-P28LKWTzrI

The Graphics Pipeline

So, how do we use these thousands of cores to generate 3D images? In brief: we set up the graphics pipeline to process vertices and textures using our shaders.[1] Figure 1 gives an overview of the graphics pipeline. This may look complicated at first, but we can break it down into logical sections.

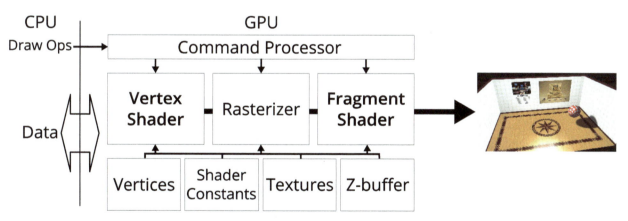

Figure 1: Overview of the Modern Graphics Pipeline

---

1   Don't worry about definitions for terms such as pipeline, vertices, etc., just yet; I'll define them later.

The Shader Pipeline

Let's start with the shader pipeline, which is the centre row in Figure 1 above. This is the heart of the system. It's called a pipeline because it takes in data at one end, runs it through multiple steps, and outputs rendered images out the other end. There are two programmable shader stages in the pipeline (the vertex and fragment shaders), and a rasterizer.[2]

The pipeline starts with the vertex shader. It takes in vertices and projects them onto the screen.

Next, the rasterizer takes the projected vertices, and "rasterizes" the triangles/lines/points (a.k.a., "primitives") they describe into pixels.

The fragment shader is executed for each of the pixels that the rasterizer generates. It's responsible for calculating the final colour for each pixel.

The shader pipeline is set up by telling the GPU which shaders to use, and configuring a few other options such as blending modes (which I've left out of the diagram for brevity).

Data

After setting up the shader pipeline, the next task is to provide the data it needs (bottom row in Figure 1). The vertex shader needs an array of vertices while fragment shaders often read textures. Both shaders can have various constants (called "uniform variables" in OpenGL). Finally, there's a z-/depth-buffer which is used to ensure that objects closest to the camera are drawn over the top of things that are farther away.

Each of the different types of data are stored in buffers. For example, vertices are typically stored in Vertex Buffer Objects (VBOs) whereas textures are stored in texture objects.

NOTE: You may encounter other buffer types as well (e.g., Shader Storage Buffer Objects). The basic principle remains the same.

The buffers are set up by first creating VBOs, textures, etc., and then loading in the data.

---

2 Shader pipelines can contain other shaders too, but we won't worry about them yet. At the bare minimum, a pipeline has a vertex and fragment shader.

The Command Processor

Okay, so you've set up the shader pipeline, and created a bunch of data objects filled with your 3D models, textures and constants. Now you can finally get the GPU to do something. This is done via the command processor.

Actually, there's one more step. You have to tell the GPU which data buffers to read from. This is done by binding the buffers to various points. For example, textures get bound to texture units. Vertex data is a bit more complicated, since each vertex can have multiple attributes (more about that later). So, the GPU is instructed to read the attributes from one or more VBOs.

We send streams of commands to the GPU via its command processor. These commands perform both the data and shader pipeline setup described above, and also the actual rendering. Graphics drivers handle all of the low-level details, so this is largely invisible.

Shaders

Shaders are specialized computer programs that run on the GPU. These are typically written in a language such as openGL Shading Language (GLSL), which is a C-like language designed specifically for graphics. Exactly what they do depends on the shader type, but the ultimate goal is to generate awesome looking rendered images.

As mentioned earlier, shaders are assembled into a pipeline, an example of which is shown in Figure 2 below. Here, there are two shaders. The vertex shader reads in the vertices and transforms them to 2D points. From there, the rasterizer converts the triangle(s) described by the vertices into pixels on-screen. The fragment shader is then run for each pixel, and it outputs the final colour.

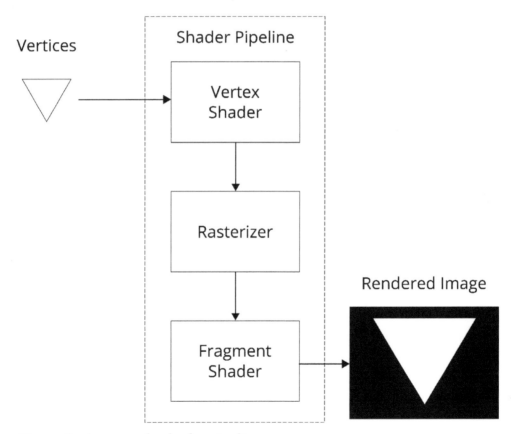

Figure 2: An example shader pipeline

Vertex Shaders

As the name suggests, vertex shader process vertices.[3] 3D models are built out of a mesh of polygons (usually triangles). Each triangle has a set of vertices. The model's vertices are usually in a local coordinate system,[4] and it's the vertex shader's task to project them onto the screen.

Vertex shaders may also perform other calculations. Typical additional tasks include:

- Passing texture coordinates on to the fragment shader

- Transforming surface normals

- Preliminary lighting calculations for per-pixel lighting (e.g., calculate the light and eye vectors)

- Skeletal animation (warping a model's mesh to generate different poses)

The projected vertices are passed on to a rasterizer to be turned into a list of pixels.

Fragment Shaders

Fragment shaders are run once for each pixel (or sub-pixel when anti-aliasing). Their task is to calculate the final surface colour for each pixel. This usually involves reading surface colours/properties from textures and performing lighting calculations.

There are countless different ways of performing lighting calculations. You may, for example, be going for photorealistic results and use physically based rendering techniques. Or, you may want a cartoon look, in which case your fragment shaders would look very different.

It's also possible to perform other calculations. For example, I used fragment shaders to perform real-time computer vision processing in my Ph.D. thesis.[5] It can also be used for image processing, and 3D rendered image post-processing (e.g., adding lens flares, motion blur, etc.).

---

3   A vertex is the corner of a triangle/polygon. It can also be defined as the point where two or more lines meet.
4   See the on page 19 for more about coordinate systems.
5   H. de Ruiter, "3D-Tracking of A Priori Unknown Objects in Cluttered Dynamic Environments," 2008, link: http://www.mie.utoronto.ca/.

Other Shaders

Other shader types also exist, and can be used for even more complex operations. Here's a quick list of what they are and what they're for.

WARNING: Getting your head around how to use everything together effectively can be challenging. Don't worry if you can't visualize how to use these shaders yet. You'll figure that out later, as you build up your expertise. Besides, you can do a lot with just vertex and fragment shaders.

Geometry Shaders

Requires: OpenGL (ES) 3.2, or GL_ARB_geometry_shader4/GL_EXT_geometry_shader

Sits between the vertex (or tessellation) shader and the rasterizer. It takes in points/lines/triangles, and can output multiple points/lines/triangles. For example, it could generate a bunch of triangles for a set of points (for point-cloud rendering). It's also used for something called shadow volume extrusion,[6] and other tasks (e.g., surface normal calculation).

While it's technically possible to tessellate (subdivide) surfaces into more detailed surfaces, this is best done using tessellation shaders, which are described below.

Tessellation Shaders

Requires OpenGL 4.0, OpenGL ES 3.2, or GL_ARB_tessellation_shader

Imagine you're rendering a landscape. There's no point in rendering mountains off in the distance with the same detail as objects that are up close; you simply can't see the detail. This is where tessellation comes in.[7]

The tessellation shaders sub-divide surfaces into smaller patches. There are actually two shaders:

- Tessellation Control Shader (TCS) – determines how much tessellation to do (i.e., how much detail to generate)

---

6   Chap. 11, Hubert Nguyen, "GPU Gems 3", http://http.developer.nvidia.com/GPUGems3/gpugems3_ch11.html.
7   Other techniques are also used to render far away landscapes at lower detail (look up "terrain level-of-detail" for more.

NOTE: This shader is optional; default tessellation parameters can be used

- Tessellation Evaluation Shader (TES) – calculates the vertex positions (and attributes) for the newly generated triangles.

There's also a "tessellation engine" between these two shaders. It performs the actual subdivision based on the parameters given it by the TCS.

Compute Shader

This is an odd-ball shader that bypasses the graphics pipeline altogether. It's used for computing arbitrary data. Example uses are:

- Perform physics simulations on the GPU

- Raytracing

- Advanced pre-processing for lighting (e.g., ambient occlusion)

- Anything well suited to processing in parallel

The data processed by a compute shader can be used by the other shaders in rendering (e.g., to render the results of a physics simulation).

The Data

As explained in the overview section (page 5), shaders read data in from several data buffers. These are:

- Vertex buffers

- Index buffers

- Textures

- Constants/Uniform variables

Details of each are given below.

Vertex Buffers

In real-time graphics objects are typically modelled as a mesh of triangles. This mesh is described by a big array of vertices,[8] and possibly an index array (more about that in the next section on page 14). For example, Figure 3 shows the Stanford Bunny's mesh.[9]

---

8   Vertices are the triangle corners.
9   https://en.wikipedia.org/wiki/Stanford_bunny

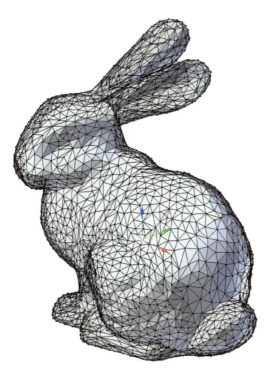

Figure 3: 3D models are typically a mesh of triangles.

Vertices are more than just points in 3D space; they can have other properties too, known as *vertex attributes*. Some typical attributes are:

- Surface normal – used for lighting calculations (see the 0 section on page 28 for more)

- Texture coordinates – for wrapping textures around the model for added detail (see the section on page 15 for more)

Figure 4 shows an example vertex array containing multiple attributes.

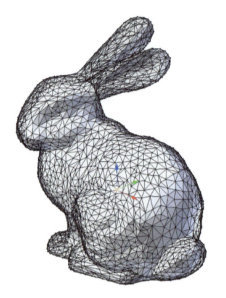

Vertex Array

0	pos0	normal0	tex-coord0
1	pos1	normal1	tex-coord1
2	pos2	normal2	tex-coord2
⋮	⋮	⋮	⋮

Figure 4: A vertex array containing position, surface normal and texture coordinate attributes.

Vertices are stored relative to the model's own coordinate system. I don't want to get into 3D transformations just yet, but there's a good reason for each model having its own coordinate system. The model's coordinates are usually centred about a point within the model (e.g., the model's centre). This makes moving the model about the world so much easier. Want to move the model? Simply update its transformation matrix.

OpenGL allows you to use vertex arrays stored in memory. However, it's highly recommended that you store the array in Video RAM (VRAM) using Vertex Buffer Objects (VBOs). This gives the GPU very high-speed access to them, improving performance. See the section on page 35 for more.

Index Arrays

Most vertices in a 3D mesh belong to multiple triangles. It would be a waste of memory to store the same vertex multiple times (once for each triangle). This is where index arrays come in.

As the name suggests, index arrays refer to vertices by index. Have a look at Figure 5. The mesh has two triangles which share two vertices. The index array has six entries that refer to the four vertices, forming the two triangles. As you can see, referencing vertices by a single index uses less memory than having duplicate copies.

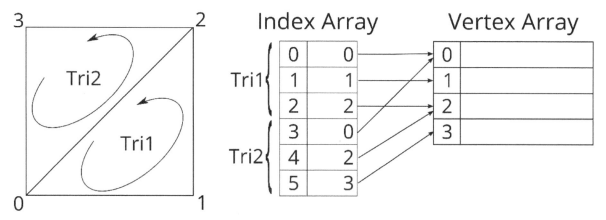

Figure 5: The index array builds a mesh by selecting vertices from a vertex array.

As with vertex arrays, index arrays are best stored in Index Buffer Objects (IBOs) so that the graphics driver can store them in VRAM for performance.

Texture Mapping

We've all wrapped presents in colourful wrapping paper. Well, texture mapping is a similar idea. You take an image and wrap it around a model. This is an easy way to add lots more detail without needing to add a huge number of vertices to the model. In Figure 6 a plain white cube becomes a wooden crate when a crate texture is wrapped around it.

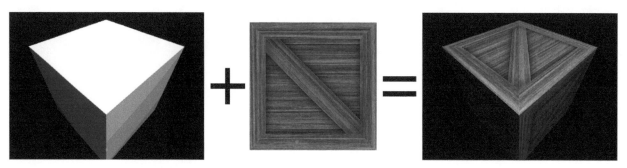

Figure 6: Texture-mapping adds detail by wrapping images (a.k.a., textures) around 3D models.

GPUs have multiple texture units, allowing you to use multiple textures for one model/mesh. This is called *multi-texturing*. This allows you to perform even more advanced effects. For example, you may add a normal map to add bumps and roughness to the surface (see the section on page 28 for more). Or maybe you have a specularity map so the surface has both shiny and dull areas. There are plenty of possible uses.

Texture Wrapping

Textures have multiple parameters that can be tweaked (via *glTexParameter*()/ glSamplerParameter*()* in OpenGL). Texture wrapping is the most interesting one. The wrapping mode decides what happens when texture coordinates go beyond the edge. There are three options:

1. *GL_REPEAT* – the texture is repeated, just like wrapping paper (Figure 7(a))

2. *GL_MIRRORED_REPEAT* – the texture is repeated, but each tile is a mirror image of the tile next to it (Figure 7(b))

3. *GL_CLAMP_TO_EDGE* – the texture is clamped to the texel on the border (Figure 7(c))

4. *GL_CLAMP_TO_BORDER* – the outside is set to a border colour (requires OpenGL ES 3.2, or GL_EXT_border_color) (Figure 7(d))

NOTE: Desktop OpenGL has a few extra options too.

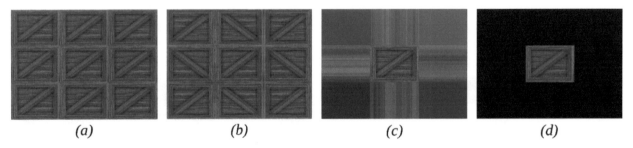

(a)   *(b)*   *(c)*   *(d)*

Figure 7: Texture wrapping modes: (a) GL_REPEAT, (b) GL_MIRRORED_REPEAT, (c) GL_CLAMP_TO_EDGE, and (d) GL_CLAMP_TO_BORDER.

Textures actually have two types of parameters: texture parameters and sampler parameters. Sampler parameters determine how the texture is read and filtered. Texture wrapping is a sampler parameter. This distinction is important because modern OpenGL allows for separate texture-sampler objects. So the same texture can be sampled different ways simultaneously.

Texture Filtering/Smoothing

Another important texture parameter (well, texture sampling parameter), is texture filtering. The filtering parameters decide what happens when a texture is magnified (enlarged) or minified (scaled down).

Filtering for enlargement is most easily understood. There are two options:

1. *GL_NEAREST* – use the closest texel; results in a blocky look (Figure 8(a))[10]

2. *GL_LINEAR* – perform linear interpolation; looks smooth but can be blurry (Figure 8(b))

(a)   (b)

Figure 8: Texture magnify filtering: (a) GL_NEAREST, and (b) GL_LINEAR.

NOTE: Texture magnification filtering is set using the *GL_TEXTURE_MAG_FILTER* in OpenGL.

---

10 Kingfisher image from: https://pixabay.com/en/kingfisher-bird-wildlife-macro-2046453/

Mipmapping

Texture minification (scaling down) is more complicated. Yes, linear filtering (*GL_LINEAR*) is still an option, but the results are less than satisfactory. The problem is that scaling down by a large amount takes a fair bit of processing power to do correctly. *GL_LINEAR* only scales down well by a factor of 2. Go over 2× reduction, and aliasing can occur.

Aliasing occurs when high detail is rendered at a resolution that's too low, resulting in weird artefacts. In technical terms, high-frequency detail is appears as low-resolution detail that's not actually there (i.e., there's a low-resolution alias). This can be seen in Figure 10(a).

This is where mipmapping comes in. With mipmapping, the texture stores scaled down copies of the full sized image. The GPU uses the copies closest to the scale that is being rendered.

Each mipmap's dimensions is half that of the previous one (Figure 9). For example, if the base texture is 256×256 pixels, then the first mipmap is 128×128, the next is 64×64, then 32×32, etc.

The effect of mipmapping can be seen by comparing Figure 10(a) and (b). Figure 10(a) uses plain linear filtering (*GL_LINEAR*), resulting in aliasing. Switching the minification filter to mipmapping (*GL_LINEAR_MIPMAP_LINEAR*) eliminates the artifacts, as seen in Figure 10(b).

You may have noticed that Figure 10(b) looks a little blurry. This occurs at sharp perspectives such as the one shown. The image would look sharp if you were facing the checkered floor head on instead of at an angle.

Figure 9: Each mipmap's dimensions are half the size of the previous one.

I don't want to get into the nitty-gritty of why it becomes blurry. Instead, I'll point to a GPU feature that combats it. It's called anisotropic filtering, and it's available in OpenGL as an (optional) extension called GL_EXT_texture_filter_anisotropic. This helps combat the blurriness, as can be seen in Figure 10(c). It's still not perfect, but definitely looks a lot better.

There are four mipmapping modes:

1. *GL_NEAREST_MIPMAP_NEAREST* – pick the closest mipmap, and then use *GL_NEAREST* within that mipmap (so pick the closest texel)

2. *GL_LINEAR_MIPMAP_NEAREST* – pick the closest mipmap, and then use *GL_LINEAR* filtering within that mipmap

3. GL_NEAREST_MIPMAP_LINEAR – chooses the closest two mipmaps, uses *GL_NEAREST* to pick the closest texel on each, and performs a weighted average between the two

4. GL_LINEAR_MIPMAP_LINEAR – performs full trilinear filtering, i.e., linearly interpolates the closest two mipmaps, and performs a weighted average between the two

NOTE: Texture minification filtering is set using the *GL_TEXTURE_MIN_FILTER* in OpenGL.

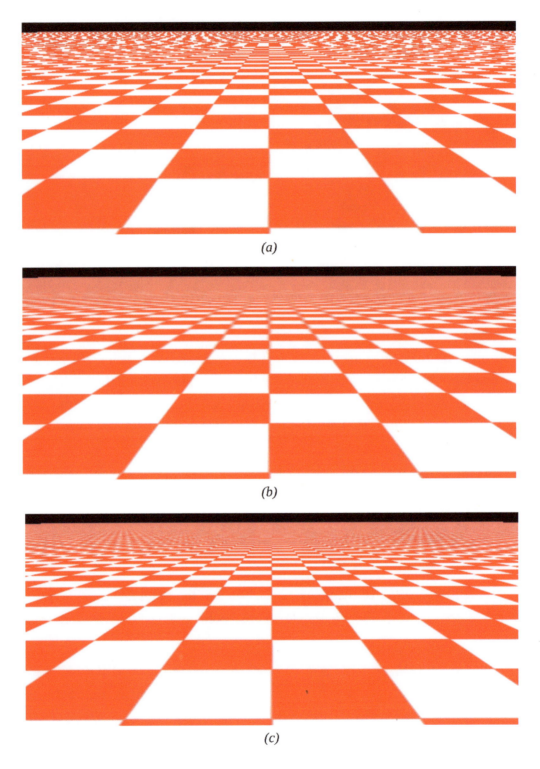

(a)

(b)

(c)

Figure 10: Different filtering modes: (a) plain linear filtering, (b) mipmapping, and (c) mipmapping with anisotropic filtering.

Constants (a.k.a., Uniform Variables)

Shader uniform variables (uniforms) store data that's common to all vertices/pixels. For example, a vertex shader usually has a Model-View-Projection (MVP) matrix that all vertices are transformed by. This is stored in a uniform variable. Here's a brief list of typical uniform variables:

- Transformation and projection matrices

- Light positions and properties

- Material properties

- Other common data

Uniforms cannot be changed by the shader; they're a constant. Calling them a variable when they're constant may seem odd. Indeed, Direct3D calls them shader constants. However, they can change between render operations. For example, a rendered object can be moved, meaning that the MVP matrix gets updated.

Whatever terminology you use, just remember that uniforms/shader-constants can be updated between render operations, but are constant as far as shaders are concerned.

The Z/Depth Buffer

The z/depth buffer is critical for correctly drawing objects that are closer in front of those that are farther away. Without it, surfaces would have to be drawn starting with those farthest away first. Otherwise you'd end up with images such as Figure 11(a).

To fix this, the GPU stores the distance to the surface for each pixel in a z/depth buffer (Figure 11(c)). Every new surface that's drawn is compared to what's been drawn before at every pixel. If it's closer, then it's drawn; otherwise it's thrown away because it's not visible. That way, objects that are closer always appear in front of those farther away, regardless of which order they're drawn in. The end result is Figure 11(b) which, I'm sure you'll agree looks a lot better than Figure 11(a).

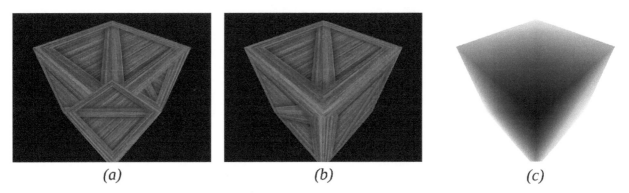

Figure 11: A cube rendered (a) without depth testing, (b) with depth testing, and (c) the resulting depth buffer (darker means closer).

3D Transformations and Coordinate Systems

To render a convincing 3D scene, objects must be projected onto a 2D screen via a simulated camera. Each object has its own position and orientation (a.k.a., pose) in the virtual world, as does the camera. So, a model's triangles/surfaces must be transformed through multiple spaces before they finally become pixels on a screen, as can be seen in Figure 12.

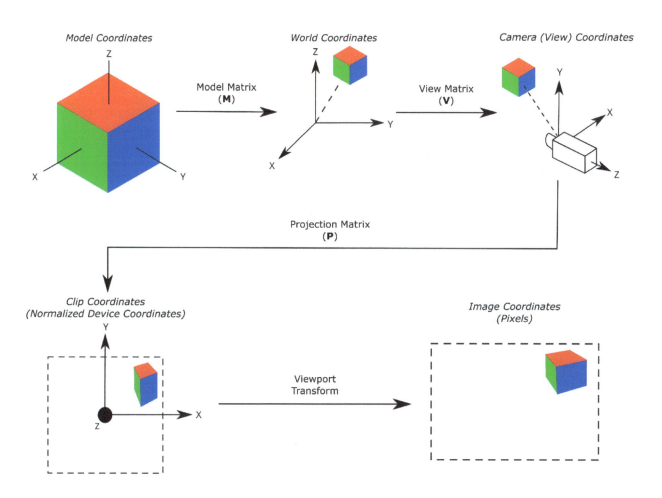

Figure 12: 3D models go through multiple transformations before being displayed on-screen.

The Model Matrix

As I said earlier, each object has a position and orientation (pose) in 3D space. The object's shape is built out of vertices and triangle's,[11] and our 3D renderer needs to project those vertices onto the screen. The first step is the model matrix.

The model matrix (**M**) stores the object's pose. Actually, that's not quite true; it's a 3D transformation. Multiplying vertex positions by the model matrix transforms them from object space to world coordinates:

$$\mathbf{p_w} = \mathbf{M}\mathbf{p_o}$$

So vertex point $\mathbf{p_o}$ is multiplied by model matrix **M** which transforms that point to its location in world space, $\mathbf{p_w}$. This is exactly what our renderer needs to do. So it's the object's pose stored in a format that the renderer can use directly (see below in Figure 13).

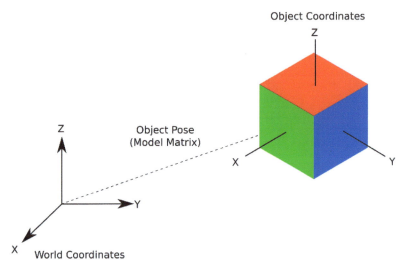

*Figure 13: The object's pose as given by the model matrix (**M**).*

---

11 NOTE: 3D models don't have to be built using vertices and triangles, but this is the most common method for graphics, especially real-time graphics such as in games.

The View Matrix

Having vertices in world space is nice, but we really need to know where they are relative to the camera. So they need to be transformed again. This is where the view matrix (**V**) comes in (Figure 14).

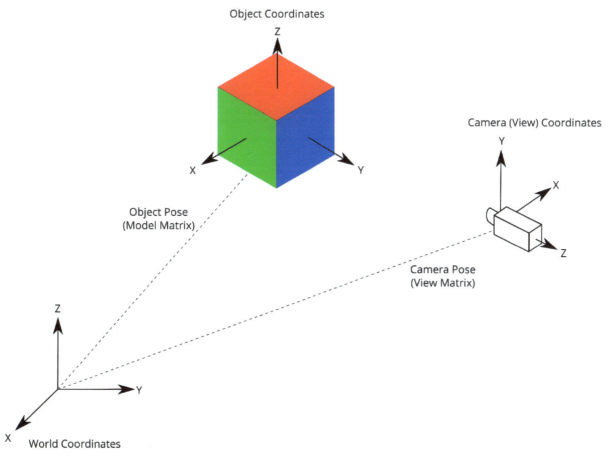

Figure 14: The object and camera's poses are given by the model and view matrices.

The view matrix transforms vertices from world to camera coordinates. Like the model matrix, it represents the camera's pose. However, it's the inverse transformation compared to the model matrix, because it transforms points *from* world coordinates instead of to world coordinates.

Multiplying by both the model and view matrices transforms vertices from model coordinates into camera coordinates:

$$\mathbf{p_v} = \mathbf{VMp_o}$$

Here, $\mathbf{V}$ is the view matrix and $\mathbf{p_v}$ is point $\mathbf{p_o}$ relative to the camera's origin (i.e., in camera coordinates).

Projection Matrix

The projection matrix is the virtual camera's lens. It projects vertices into clip space (also called Normalized Device Coordinates (NDC)). This is a two step process. First $\mathbf{p_v}$ is multiplied by the projection matrix ($\mathbf{P}$):

$$\mathbf{p_c} = \mathbf{Pp_v} = \mathbf{PVMp_o}$$

The result is a vector with the following values:

- x - the horizontal position
- y - the vertical position
- z - the depth value
- w - the actual distance to the point along the z-axis

Next, 3D to 2D projection is performed by dividing all values above by w.

Why clip space? Well, clip space makes it easy for the GPU to discard any points that are not visible. All visible points lie within a unit cube (i.e., x, y, & z values lie within the range [-1,1]).[12] Triangles completely outside the clip cube can't be seen by the camera, and are discarded. There's no point in wasting any more processing power on something that the camera can't see.

The Special Z and the Depth Buffer

It may seem strange to have both a depth value (z) and a z-axis distance (w). Aren't they the same? Not exactly. The depth value used to determine which surface is closest to the camera. Objects that are closest to the camera must always appear in front of those that are farther away.

Depth testing is performed by using a depth buffer. This buffer records the depth (z) for every pixel. When a triangle is rendered, the GPU checks whether it's closer to the camera than any previously rendered surfaces. The GPU then only draws the triangle to pixels where it's the closest to the camera.

---

12   NOTE: Direct-X and Vulkan use a z-axis clip range of [0,1] instead of [-1,1].

A separate depth value is used because the projection calculation must be done at high precision (using w) whereas the depth buffer could have limited precision (e.g., it might be 16-bit rather than 32-bit). Clipping the depth value to [-1,1] ensures that it can be scaled to fit the depth buffer regardless of precision.

The MVP Matrix

There's no point in making the GPU multiply points by each matrix separately; that's wasteful. So, the model, view and projection matrices can merged beforehand into the MVP transformation matrix:

$$\mathbf{M_{MVP}} = \mathbf{PVM}$$

That way vertices only need to be multiplied by one matrix instead of three; a 3x saving in processing power. Notice how the matrix order is from right-to-left. This is because the position vector is to the right, and so is multiplied by the right-most matrix first.

The Viewport Transform

After vertices have been clipped, they're transformed to screen/pixel coordinates. You won't need to calculate this transformation yourself because OpenGL's *glViewport()* calculates this for you.

This is the final transformation. The 3D object has been projected onto the 2D image, and can now be drawn to screen. At this point the triangles are converted to pixels, and the fragment shader is run for each pixel.

Lighting

In the real world light is emitted by the sun, lights, fires, etc. That light then passes through the air and bounces around as it interacts with objects. Some of those rays of light eventually pass through the lenses in your eyes, which focus them into images on your retinas. Your brain interprets these images, forming a mental picture of the world around you.

Theoretically, you could simulate the process of light bouncing around and interacting with matter in excruciating detail, delivering physically accurate images (i.e., do ray-tracing). That would take huge amounts of processing power, though, so we use approximate lighting models instead. It's possible to generate pretty realistic graphics this way. We're going to look at the Phong reflection model.[13]

WARNING: This section gets more mathematical than previous ones. If you have difficulty with the mathematics, then focus on the concepts behind them. See the section on page 55 for resources on vector/matrix algebra.

Phong Reflection Model

The Phong reflection model is fairly old. It isn't based directly on physics, yet produces pretty decent images (Figure 15). More importantly, it's fairly easy to understand and implement.

The Phong model divides reflections into three components: ambient, diffuse, and specular. Each approximate different phenomenon. I'm going to cover them in reverse order because I think specular lighting is the easiest to understand conceptually.

---

13 https://en.wikipedia.org/wiki/Phong_reflection_model

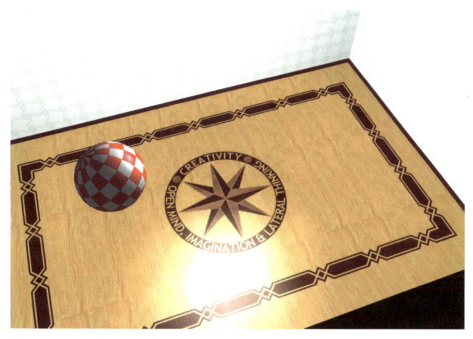

Figure 15: Phong shading generates the realistic lighting in this demo.

Specular Reflection

Specular means: "relating to or having the properties of a mirror." So we're talking about shiny surfaces such as mirrors, metals, shiny plastic, etc. A perfect reflector such as a mirror reflects light as shown below. The angle at which the reflected light leaves matches the angle that the light hit the surface (Figure 16).

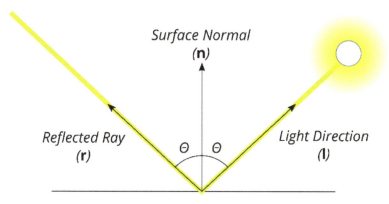

Figure 16: Perfect specular (mirror) reflection.

The surface normal (shown above) is a unit vector pointing directly out of the surface at 90 degrees (i.e., it's perpendicular to the surface). This vector is key to calculating the lighting; neither specular nor diffuse reflections can be calculated without it. "Unit vector" means that the vector has a length of 1.

Of course, not everything is a perfect reflector. With other surfaces the specular reflection may spread out slightly in a cone (see below). Actually, it's more of a fuzzy cone. Light is most intense in the cone's centre and falls off as you move outward (Figure 17).

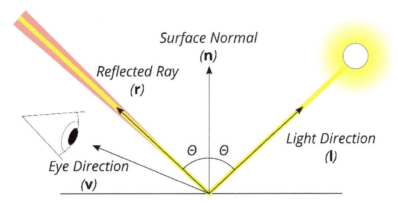

Figure 17: Imperfect specular reflection spreads light out away from the centre.

Mathematically, the specular reflection above is given by the following equation:

$$\mathbf{i_s} = \max(k_s\mathbf{i}(\mathbf{v}\cdot\mathbf{r})^s, \, 0)$$

Here:

- k_s is the specular reflection constant
- $\mathbf{i}$ is the incoming light intensity
- $\mathbf{v}$ is the direction (a.k.a., a unit vector) from the surface to the eye/camera
- $\mathbf{r}$ is the direction that the light would take in a perfect reflection
- s is the surface's shininess factor. This controls how narrow (or perfect) the reflection is. The higher the value, the narrower and more perfect the reflection

v·r is the dot-product of vectors **v** and **r**. If your unfamiliar with dot products, imagine creating a right-angle triangle using vectors **v** and **r** as shown below. The dot-product is the length along **r** to the triangle's right-angled (90 degree) corner. This is also called the "projection of **v** on **r**," but I find it easier to understand visually (Figure 18).

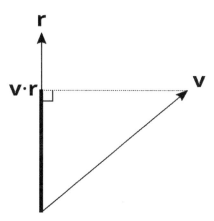

Figure 18: The dot-product is the "projection of v on r."

The formula above can't be used directly, as we don't have the reflection direction (**r**) yet. This is calculated from the normal (**n**) and light direction (**l**) vectors as follows:

r = *2(**n·l**)**n** - **l***

The formula above can be derived visually as shown in Figure 19 below. Basically, go along the normal vector **n** by *2(**n·l**)*, and then subtract the light vector **l**; now you have the reflection vector **r**.

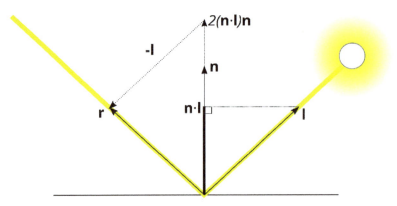

Figure 19: Visually calculating the reflection vector from the light and normal vectors.

The function *max()* ensures that the light intensity cannot go negative. "Negative light" means that the light is coming from behind the surface, which is invisible. This occurs when $\mathbf{n}\cdot\mathbf{l} < 0$.

Diffuse Reflection

An object with a rough surface will scatter light in all directions (Figure 20). This is called diffuse reflection. I'm talking about microscopic roughness too small to see with the naked eye.

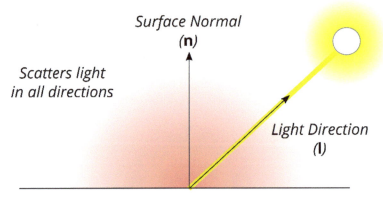

Figure 20: Diffuse light scatters in all directions.

The light intensity depends on the angle at which light hits the surface, which is modelled via the following formula:

$\mathbf{i_d} = max(k_d\mathbf{i}(\mathbf{n}\cdot\mathbf{l}),\ 0)$

k_d is the diffuse reflection constant, and $\mathbf{i_d}$ is the reflected light intensity. The other symbols (e.g., $\mathbf{n}$ & $\mathbf{l}$) are the same as for the specular reflection formula.

Did you notice that the formula above doesn't depend on the eye/view vector $\mathbf{v}$? That's because light is scattered equally in all directions, so only the surface normal ($\mathbf{n}$) and light position ($\mathbf{l}$) matter.

Ambient Light

The specular & diffuse light equations above handle light hitting surfaces directly from its source. However, light is more complicated than that. Light that bounces off one surface can hit another surface, reflect off that and hit another, and another, etc. This "indirect illumination" affects the final colour we see. We call this ambient light.

The Phong lighting model pretends that this background scattering is uniform across the scene. That's not true in reality. Try the following: put a bright red object like a ball or book on top of a piece of white paper. Now look carefully at the white paper close to the ball. You'll see a reddish tinge. That's reflected red light from the ball hitting the white paper.

Reducing ambient light to a single constant is a quick-n-dirty approximation. It's often "good enough" even if it's technically incorrect. There are techniques to handle ambient light more accurately, but they tend to be complicated and computationally intensive. Look up "Global Illumination" if you're curious. In any case, here's the Phong ambient light formula:

$\mathbf{i_a} = k_a\mathbf{i}$

k_a is the ambient reflection constant, and $\mathbf{i_a}$ is the reflected ambient light intensity.

Putting it All Together

Specular, diffuse and ambient reflection's aren't mutually exclusive. Plenty of objects have a shiny outer layer over the top of a diffuse reflecting under-layer. So a surface can have both specular and diffuse reflections. That's how you see a shiny reflection on a red snooker ball, for example. The ambient component is a special case, because it's really a fudge factor to approximate the effect of many interreflections. So, to get the final surface colour, we simply add everything together:

$$\mathbf{i_s} = max(k_s\mathbf{i}(\mathbf{v \cdot r})^s,\ 0) + max(k_d\mathbf{i}(\mathbf{n \cdot l}),\ 0) + k_a\mathbf{i}$$

$\mathbf{i_s}$ is the surface colour, as viewed by the eye/camera. Multiple lights can be handled simply by adding the specular, diffuse, and ambient reflections from all lights together.

Point Lights

Bet you thought we were done, eh? Not quite. The distance that a light is from the surface also has an effect, as does the light's type. There are various light source types, such as point lights, area lights, and spot-lights. Each have different attenuation[14] formulae. I'm only going to go into point lights here. You're welcome to look up the properties of other light types.

Point lights are used to approximate things such as small light bulbs. Ideal point lights don't really exist; lights always have a non-zero size. However, approximating them as a point usually works well.

Light attenuates (falls away) from a point light source as the inverse square of the distance, so:

$$i = \frac{i_s}{d^2}$$

Here, $\mathbf{i_s}$ is the base light intensity (as an RGB colour), and d is the distance from the light.

The inverse square law has one undesirable property: it approaches infinity as the distance goes to zero. So, it's common to use alternative formulae such as:

$$i = i_s clamp\left(1 - \frac{d^2}{r^2}, 0, 1\right)^2$$

Here, r is the distance from the light at which the light intensity should be 0. The *clamp()* function restricts the attenuation to the range [0,1]. This gives a reasonable approximation with the advantage that you can set the maximum distance where the light has any effect.

---

14 Attenuation: reduction in the light's intensity.

Performance

As with general programming, there are various bottlenecks that can restrict performance. Know what they are, and you can get better performance out of the GPU. Some (but not all) of the key bottlenecks are shown in Figure 21. These are:

- Draw-calls/s – there's a maximum number of draw calls/s that the GPU can manage

- Data transfer (GiB/s) – the bus connecting the CPU and GPU has a maximum transfer rate, which can affect both the draw ops/s and how much data (vertices, textures, etc.) can be transferred

- Shader ops/s – the GPU's shader cores have a maximum number of instructions per second they can perform, so complex shaders will take longer

- Vertices/s – there is a maximum number of vertices/s that can be fetched, even when they're stored in VRAM

- VRAM bandwidth – video memory also has a maximum transfer rate (affects the vertices/s, texels/s and fill rate)

- Texels/s – the GPU can only process so many texels a second

- Fill rate (pixels/s) – the maximum number of pixels/s that the GPU can render

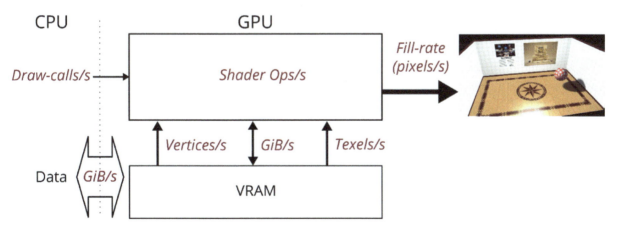

Figure 21: Some key bottlenecks that can limit performance.

Performance optimization is a complicated and specialist topic. Nevertheless, here are some basic guidelines that give quick wins.

Use Vertex Buffer Objects (VBOs)

OpenGL gives you the option of using vertex arrays in main memory. It's quick-n-easy, but also consumes bus bandwidth because the GPU must read across the PCI-Express bus to main memory. You're highly likely to hit the data transfer bottleneck with this.

Using VBOs allows the GPU to copy the vertices into VRAM, which the GPU has much higher speed access to. As a result, the maximum number of vertices/s increases.

There is one caveat to this. Sometimes you may have models/vertices that the CPU modifies every frame (i.e., you're streaming data). In this case, main memory is the best location. However, you should still use VBOs because the driver can store those in main memory too. Simply let the driver know that the buffer will be used for streamed data. In OpenGL, calling *glBufferData()* with *GL_STREAM_DRAW* will allocate a buffer that's optimised for streaming data to the GPU. Likewise, *GL_STATIC_DRAW* is for buffers with data that won't change (and should therefore be stored in VRAM).

NOTE: It's better to use glBufferSubData() when updating an existing buffer. This is usually faster, because you can update just the bits that change and it doesn't reallocate the buffer (as glBufferData() may).

Draw as Much as You Can in a Single Draw Call

There's a limit to how many draw-calls/s the computer can manage. As a general principle, try to draw as much as possible per draw call. It's possible to pack multiple objects into one buffer, and use a technique called instanced rendering to render multiple objects with different parameters (e.g., using *glDrawElementsInstanced()*).

There are actually multiple factors that create this draw-calls/s limit. One is the overhead per draw call, but there's also a cost to switching between buffers, textures, and other state changes. Its also generally faster to perform a few large buffer updates vs many small ones.

The bottom line is, try to draw as much as possible in as few draw calls as possible. And, also try render things in an order that minimises state changes (e.g., draw multiple items with the same material together before switching textures for the next group of items).

Don't Clear the Colour Buffer Unless Absolutely Necessary

If you're rendering 3D scenes (or even 2D ones), then it's very likely that you'll overwrite all pixels every frame. If so, then it's a complete waste of time to clear them all first. You will have to clear the depth buffer (and maybe the stencil buffer), but don't bother clearing the colour buffer. For example, in OpenGL, *glClear(GL_DEPTH_BUFFER_BIT)* clears just the depth-buffer.

IMPORTANT: For this to work you really need to draw to every single pixel. This is guaranteed if you have a skybox or full screen background.

Render Objects Roughly in Front-to-Back Order

Imagine you had 1000 cubes positioned one behind another. If you drew them in back-to-front order, then each cube would be drawn, only to be overwritten by the cube in front. This is called *overdraw*, and it's a huge waste.

Rendering objects in front-to-back order minimises how many times each pixel is written to. This can save a lot of processing power and VRAM bandwidth, thereby improving performance.

Caveats

Of course, things aren't quite so simple. For starters, sorting objects takes time, and some objects may overlap. Hence, the goal is to render *roughly* in front-to-back order. There's definitely no reason to be sorting every single triangle. You don't want the time spent sorting objects to outweigh the time savings from reducing overdraw.

Secondly, you may need to render some objects in back-to-front order to handle effects such as transparency. With transparency, the object(s) behind are visible through the transparent object. So, those objects still need to be drawn, and often need to be drawn first.

Only Render Objects that are Potentially Visible

Every draw operation costs time, even if nothing is drawn. So, it makes sense to only draw things that are visible. This is one of the key techniques allow sophisticated graphics engines to render large and complex worlds. At any given time, the engine only draws objects that are potentially visible.

The phrase "potentially visible" might strike you as odd. Why not only objects that are visible? Well, calculating visibility takes processing power too. The more accurate you calculate the visibility, the more processing time it consumes. At some point, the cost of calculating visibility wipes out all savings gained by reducing the number of objects that are drawn.

How does one go about calculating approximate visibility efficiently? Well, your 3D world needs to be subdivided into regions. Then only objects in regions the camera can see need be drawn.

There are multiple different space subdivision techniques. A few are: portals, octrees, Binary Space Partitioning, and kd-trees. Each has their own pros and cons, and work best under certain conditions (e.g., portals work well for indoor scenes but are a poor choice for outdoors).

The details of these space subdivision techniques is beyond the scope of this primer. Focus on the basics of rendering first, and worry about how to render large-scale worlds later. Once you've mastered rendering, then you can look into these techniques.

There's Lot's More

As you delve deeper into the world of computer graphics you'll discover a multitude of techniques. In addition to topics already covered, you'll probably hear things like:

- Skeletal animation

- Shadow volumes & shadow mapping

- Deferred shading

- Level-of-detail algorithms

- Scene-graphs

- Megatextures/sparse-virtual-textures

- Raytracing and raycasting

- Voxel rendering

- Screen-Space Ambient Occlusion (SSAO) and other ambient occlusion techniques

- Physical based rendering

Researchers are coming up with innovative new techniques all the time. It's easy to get lost in the sea of possibilities.

When starting out it's important to stick to the basics. Master the core fundamentals first, and then start branching out into more advanced techniques. This primer and the accompanying tutorial series are a good starting point. See the section on page 55 for resources to learn further.

If you're dreaming about writing your own computer games, then please please *please*, focus on gameplay first. Making it fun to play is more important than how flashy the graphics is. It's always a shame when a game looks visually impressive but is kind of boring or annoying to play.[15] Simple graphics is often more than enough for a good game, although realistic rendering can definitely help make a game more immersive.

---

15 "Rise of the Robots" is a good example of a game with impressive graphics, but poor gameplay: https://en.wikipedia.org/wiki/Rise_of_the_Robots#Reception.

OpenGL ES 3+ & SDL2 Cheat-Sheet

This section gives code snippets for various basic tasks. It uses OpenGL ES 3+ with SDL2 (plus SDL_image) and GLM (for vector/matrix mathematics). This is currently my preferred combination, and is what the accompanying tutorial series uses.

Basic Window and Event Handling

Includes

The following #includes cover everything needed for the code snippets:

```
#include <SDL.h>
#include <SDL_image.h>
#include <SDL_opengles2.h>
#include <GLES3/gl3.h>
#include <glm/glm.hpp>
#include <glm/gtc/matrix_inverse.hpp>
#include <glm/gtc/matrix_transform.hpp>
#include <glm/gtc/type_ptr.hpp>
#include <glm/gtx/transform.hpp>
```

Creating an OpenGL (ES 3.0) Window

```
    // The window
    SDL_Window *window = NULL;

    // The OpenGL context
    SDL_GLContext context = NULL;

    // Init SDL
    if (SDL_Init(SDL_INIT_VIDEO) < 0) {
        SDL_Log("SDL could not initialize! SDL_Error: %s\n", SDL_GetError());
        return EXIT_FAILURE;
    }

    // Setup the exit hook
    atexit(SDL_Quit);

    // Request OpenGL ES 3.0
    SDL_GL_SetAttribute(SDL_GL_CONTEXT_PROFILE_MASK,
```

```
        SDL_GL_CONTEXT_PROFILE_ES);
SDL_GL_SetAttribute(SDL_GL_CONTEXT_MAJOR_VERSION, 3);
SDL_GL_SetAttribute(SDL_GL_CONTEXT_MINOR_VERSION, 0);

// Force usage of the GLES backend
SDL_SetHint(SDL_HINT_OPENGL_ES_DRIVER, "1");

// Want double-buffering
SDL_GL_SetAttribute(SDL_GL_DOUBLEBUFFER, 1);

// Create the window
window = SDL_CreateWindow("GLES3+SDL2 Tutorial", SDL_WINDOWPOS_UNDEFINED,
    SDL_WINDOWPOS_UNDEFINED, DISP_WIDTH, DISP_HEIGHT, SDL_WINDOW_OPENGL
    SDL_WINDOW_SHOWN);
if (!window) {
    SDL_ShowSimpleMessageBox(SDL_MESSAGEBOX_ERROR, "Error",
        "Couldn't create the main window.", NULL);
    return EXIT_FAILURE;
}

context = SDL_GL_CreateContext(window);
if (!context) {
    SDL_ShowSimpleMessageBox(SDL_MESSAGEBOX_ERROR, "Error",
        "Couldn't create an OpenGL context.", NULL);
    return EXIT_FAILURE;
}
```

Create a 24-/32-bit FrameBuffer

SDL2 may choose to create a 16-bit framebuffer, which reduces the visual quality a bit (can cause visible banding). While this may be a good thing on mobile phones where resources are more limited,[16] a 24-/32-bit framebuffer looks better. Here's how to request it:

```
SDL_GL_SetAttribute(SDL_GL_RED_SIZE, 8);
SDL_GL_SetAttribute(SDL_GL_GREEN_SIZE, 8);
SDL_GL_SetAttribute(SDL_GL_BLUE_SIZE, 8);
```

---

16 A 16-bit buffer consumes less memory and bandwidth, which can improve performance or at least reduce battery consumption.

NOTE: Put this with the other *SDL_GL_SetAttribute()* calls (see the Create a Window section above).

Flip Buffers to Display New Image

```
// Update the window
SDL_GL_SwapWindow(window);
```

Main Loop

This is a very basic main loop that polls events, performs animation/simulation, and renders the next frame:

```
// The main loop
bool quit = false;
Uint32 prevTime = SDL_GetTicks();
while (!quit) {
    // Handle events
    SDL_Event event;
    if (SDL_PollEvent(&event) != 0) {
        if (event.type == SDL_QUIT) {
            // User wants to quit
            quit = true;
        }
        // ##### INSERT OTHER EVENT HANDLERS #####
    }

    // Animate
    Uint32 currTime = SDL_GetTicks();
    float elapsedTime = (float)(currTime - prevTime) / 1000.0f;
    prevTime = currTime; // Prepare for the next frame
    // ##### INSERT ANIMATION/SIMULATION CODE #####

    // Redraw
    // ##### INSERT CODE TO RENDER THE SCENE #####

    // Update the window (flip the buffers)
    SDL_GL_SwapWindow(window);
```

```
    }
```

Using OpenGL

Set up Depth Buffer

```c
// Enable and set up the depth buffer
glEnable(GL_DEPTH_TEST);
glDepthFunc(GL_LESS);
glClearDepthf(1.0f);
```

Create and Compile a Shader

```c
// Create the shader
GLuint shader = glCreateShader(shaderType);
glShaderSource(shader, 1, (const GLchar**)&shaderSrc, NULL);
free(shaderSrc);
shaderSrc = NULL;

// Compile it
glCompileShader(shader);
GLint compileSucceeded = GL_FALSE;
glGetShaderiv(shader, GL_COMPILE_STATUS, &compileSucceeded);
if (!compileSucceeded) {
    // Compilation failed. Print error info
    SDL_Log("Compilation of shader %s failed:\n", filename);
    GLint logLength = 0;
    glGetShaderiv(shader, GL_INFO_LOG_LENGTH, &logLength);
    GLchar *errLog = (GLchar*)malloc(logLength);
    if (errLog) {
        glGetShaderInfoLog(shader, logLength, &logLength, errLog);
        SDL_Log("%s\n", errLog);
        free(errLog);
    }
    else {
        SDL_Log("Couldn't get shader log; out of memory\n");
    }

    glDeleteShader(shader);
    shader = 0;
```

}

Delete/Destroy a Shader

NOTE: You can delete a shader after creating a shader program from it (the shader program doesn't need the shader object to remain allocated).

```
glDeleteShader(shaderID);
```

Create a Shader Program

NOTE: The fragShader and vertShader variables were created using the "Create a Shader" procedure above.

```
GLuint shaderProg = glCreateProgram();
if (shaderProg) {
    glAttachShader(shaderProg, vertShader);
    glAttachShader(shaderProg, fragShader);

    glLinkProgram(shaderProg);

    GLint linkingSucceeded = GL_FALSE;
    glGetProgramiv(shaderProg, GL_LINK_STATUS, &linkingSucceeded);
    if (!linkingSucceeded) {
        SDL_Log("Linking shader failed (vert. shader: %s, frag. shader:
%s\n",
            vertFilename, fragFilename);
        GLint logLength = 0;
        glGetProgramiv(shaderProg, GL_INFO_LOG_LENGTH, &logLength);
        GLchar *errLog = (GLchar*)malloc(logLength);
        if (errLog) {
            glGetProgramInfoLog(shaderProg, logLength, &logLength,
errLog);
            SDL_Log("%s\n", errLog);
            free(errLog);
        }
        else {
            SDL_Log("Couldn't get shader link log; out of memory\n");
        }
        glDeleteProgram(shaderProg);
        shaderProg = 0;
    }
}
```

```
else {
    SDL_Log("Couldn't create shader program\n");
}

// Don't need these any more
shaderDestroy(vertShader);
shaderDestroy(fragShader);
```

Delete/Destroy Shader Program

```
glDeleteProgram(shaderProg);
```

Create a Vertex Buffer Object (VBO)

```
/** Encapsulates the data for a single vertex.
 * Must match the vertex shader's input.
 */
typedef struct Vertex_s {
    float position[3];
    float texCoord[2];
    float normal[3];
} Vertex;

/** Creates the Vertex Buffer Object (VBO) containing
 * the given vertices.
 *
 * @param vertices pointer to the array of vertices
 * @param numVertices the number of vertices in the array
 */
GLuint vboCreate(const Vertex *vertices, GLuint numVertices) {
    // Create the Vertex Buffer Object
    GLuint vbo;
    int nBuffers = 1;
    glGenBuffers(nBuffers, &vbo);
    glBindBuffer(GL_ARRAY_BUFFER, vbo);

    // Copy the vertex data in, and deactivate
    glBufferData(GL_ARRAY_BUFFER, sizeof(Vertex) * numVertices, vertices,
        GL_STATIC_DRAW);
    glBindBuffer(GL_ARRAY_BUFFER, 0);
```

```
    // Check for problems
    GLenum err = glGetError();
    if (err != GL_NO_ERROR) {
        // Failed
        glDeleteBuffers(nBuffers, &vbo);
        SDL_Log("Creating VBO failed, code %u\n", err);
        vbo = 0;
    }

    return vbo;
}
```

NOTES:

- The *Vertex* structure must match whatever vertex data your shader(s) needs

- Use *glBufferSubData()* instead of *glBufferData()* when updating an existing buffer. It's faster because it avoids buffer reallocation and allows updating just the bit you want changed

Use a VBO

```
    // Set up for rendering the model (activate the VBO)
    GLuint positionIdx = 0; // Position is vertex attribute 0
    glBindBuffer(GL_ARRAY_BUFFER, vbo);
    glVertexAttribPointer(positionIdx, 3, GL_FLOAT, GL_FALSE,
        sizeof(Vertex), (const GLvoid*)0);
    glEnableVertexAttribArray(positionIdx);
    GLuint texCoordIdx = 1;  // TexCoord is vertex attribute 1
    glVertexAttribPointer(texCoordIdx, 2, GL_FLOAT, GL_FALSE,
        sizeof(Vertex), (const GLvoid*)offsetof(Vertex, texCoord));
    glEnableVertexAttribArray(texCoordIdx);
    GLuint normalIdx = 2;  // Normal is vertex attribute 2
    glVertexAttribPointer(normalIdx, 3, GL_FLOAT, GL_FALSE,
        sizeof(Vertex), (const GLvoid*)offsetof(Vertex, normal));
    glEnableVertexAttribArray(normalIdx);
```

NOTES:

- This code matches the VBO creation code above. You'll need to adapt it to your own shader code.

- Make sure your shader uses layout(location = n) to fix the locations of each vertex attribute, e.g.:

```
#version 300 es

layout(location = 0) in vec3 vertPos;
layout(location = 1) in vec2 vertTexCoord;
layout(location = 2) in vec3 vertNormal;
```

Delete/Destroy VBO

```
glDeleteBuffers(1, &vbo);
```

Create an Index Buffer Object (IBO)

```
// Create the Index Buffer Object
GLuint ibo;
int nBuffers = 1;
glGenBuffers(nBuffers, &ibo);
glBindBuffer(GL_ELEMENT_ARRAY_BUFFER, ibo);

// Copy the index data in, and deactivate
glBufferData(GL_ELEMENT_ARRAY_BUFFER, sizeof(indices[0]) * numIndices,
    indices, GL_STATIC_DRAW);
glBindBuffer(GL_ELEMENT_ARRAY_BUFFER, 0);

// Check for problems
GLenum err = glGetError();
if (err != GL_NO_ERROR) {
    // Failed
    glDeleteBuffers(nBuffers, &ibo);
    SDL_Log("Creating IBO failed, code %u\n", err);
    ibo = 0;
}
```

Use an IBO to Draw/Render

```
// Bind the index array for use
glBindBuffer(GL_ELEMENT_ARRAY_BUFFER, ibo);

// Draw
glDrawElements(GL_TRIANGLES, numIndices, GL_UNSIGNED_SHORT, (GLvoid*)0);
```

Delete/Destroy IBO

```
glDeleteBuffers(1, &ibo);
```

Get Uniform Location

NOTE: With OpenGL 4.3+ and OpenGL ES 3.1+ this step can be skipped by setting the locations in the shader using *layout(location = n)*. Since we're targeting OpenGL ES 3.0, this is still necessary.

```
// Get other uniform locations
GLint mvMatLoc = glGetUniformLocation(shaderProg, "mvMat");
if (mvMatLoc < 0) {
    SDL_Log("ERROR: Couldn't get mvMat's location.");
    return EXIT_FAILURE;
}
```

Upload Uniform Data to GPU

This example is for uploading a matrix. Other data is uploaded using similar *glUniform*() functions.

```
mvMat = viewMat * modelMat;
glUniformMatrix4fv(mvMatLoc, 1, GL_FALSE, glm::value_ptr(mvMat));
```

Draw Something

The following clears the screen and renders an object using a previously set up VBO and IBO (remember to flip the buffers afterward):

```
// Redraw
glClear(GL_COLOR_BUFFER_BIT | GL_DEPTH_BUFFER_BIT);
glDrawElements(GL_TRIANGLES, numIndices, GL_UNSIGNED_SHORT,
```

```
        (GLvoid*)0);
```

Load a Texture From Disk

```c
/** Sets the swizzling for a texture colour channel from an SDL colour mask.
 *
 * @param channel the texture channel to set (e.g., GL_TEXTURE_SWIZZLE_R)
 * @param mask the SDL colour channel mask (e.g., texSurf->format->Rmask)
 */
bool sdlToGLSwizzle(GLenum channel, Uint32 mask) {
    GLint swizzle;
    switch (mask) {
    case 0x000000FF:
#if SDL_BYTEORDER == SDL_BIG_ENDIAN
            swizzle = GL_ALPHA;
#else
            swizzle = GL_RED;
#endif
        break;
    case 0x0000FF00:
#if SDL_BYTEORDER == SDL_BIG_ENDIAN
            swizzle = GL_BLUE;
#else
            swizzle = GL_GREEN;
#endif
        break;
    case 0x00FF0000:
#if SDL_BYTEORDER == SDL_BIG_ENDIAN
            swizzle = GL_GREEN;
#else
            swizzle = GL_BLUE;
#endif
        break;
    case 0xFF000000:
#if SDL_BYTEORDER == SDL_BIG_ENDIAN
            swizzle = GL_ALPHA;
#else
            swizzle = GL_RED;
#endif
        break;
```

```
    default:
        SDL_Log("Unrecognized colour channel mask 0x%08X", mask);
        return false;
    }

    glTexParameteri(GL_TEXTURE_2D, channel, swizzle);
    return true;
}


/** Loads a 2D texture from file.
 *
 * @param filename name of the image file to load
 *
 * @return GLuint the texture's name, or 0 if failed
 */
GLuint texLoad(const char *filename) {
    // Make sure the JPEG and PNG image loaders are present (don't know what
    // file type we'll get).
    int flags = IMG_INIT_JPG | IMG_INIT_PNG;
    if ((IMG_Init(flags) & flags) == 0) {
        // Failed :-(
        SDL_Log("ERROR: Texture loading failed. "
            "Couldn't get JPEG & PNG loaders.\n");
        return 0;
    }


    // Load the image
    SDL_Surface *texSurf = IMG_Load(filename);
    if (!texSurf) {
        SDL_Log("Loading image %s failed with error: %s",
            filename, IMG_GetError());
        return 0;
    }


    // Determine the format
    // NOTE: Only supporting 24 and 32-bit images
    GLenum format;
    GLenum type = GL_UNSIGNED_BYTE;
    switch (texSurf->format->BytesPerPixel) {
    case 3:
```

```c
            format = GL_RGB;
            break;
        case 4:
            format = GL_RGBA;
            break;
        default:
            SDL_Log("Can't load image %s; it isn't a 24/32-bit image\n",
                filename);
            SDL_FreeSurface(texSurf);
            texSurf = NULL;
            return 0;
    }

    // Create the texture
    GLuint texture;
    glGenTextures(1, &texture);
    glBindTexture(GL_TEXTURE_2D, texture);
    glTexImage2D(GL_TEXTURE_2D, 0, GL_RGBA, texSurf->w,
        texSurf->h, 0, format, type, texSurf->pixels);
    GLenum err = glGetError();
    if (err != GL_NO_ERROR) {
        // Failed
        glDeleteBuffers(1, &texture);
        texture = 0;
        SDL_FreeSurface(texSurf);
        texSurf = NULL;
        SDL_Log("Creating texture %s failed, code %u\n", filename, err);
        return 0;
    }

    // Set up texture swizzling to match the image's channel order
    bool success = sdlToGLSwizzle(GL_TEXTURE_SWIZZLE_R,
        texSurf->format->Rmask);
    success &= sdlToGLSwizzle(GL_TEXTURE_SWIZZLE_G, texSurf->format->Gmask);
    success &= sdlToGLSwizzle(GL_TEXTURE_SWIZZLE_B, texSurf->format->Bmask);
    if (format == GL_RGBA) {
        success &= sdlToGLSwizzle(GL_TEXTURE_SWIZZLE_A,
            texSurf->format->Amask);
    }
    if (!success) {
```

```
        SDL_Log("Couldn't set up swizzling for texture %s\n", filename);
        glDeleteBuffers(1, &texture);
        texture = 0;
        SDL_FreeSurface(texSurf);
        texSurf = NULL;
        return 0;
    }


    // Set up the filtering
    // NOTE: Failure to do this may result in no texture
    glTexParameteri(GL_TEXTURE_2D, GL_TEXTURE_MAG_FILTER, GL_LINEAR);
    glTexParameteri(GL_TEXTURE_2D, GL_TEXTURE_MIN_FILTER, GL_LINEAR);


    // Cleanup
    SDL_FreeSurface(texSurf);
    texSurf = NULL;


    return texture;
}
```

Set Texture Location

NOTE: With OpenGL 4.2+ and OpenGL ES 3.1+ this step can be skipped by setting the binding in the shader using *layout(binding = n)*. Since we're targeting OpenGL ES 3.0, this is still necessary.

```
    // Bind texSampler to unit 0
    GLint texSamplerUniformLoc =
        glGetUniformLocation(shaderProg, "texSampler");
    if (texSamplerUniformLoc < 0) {
        SDL_Log("ERROR: Couldn't get texSampler's location.");
        return EXIT_FAILURE;
    }
    glUniform1i(texSamplerUniformLoc, 0);
```

Use a Texture (a.k.a., Binding to Texture Unit)

```
    // Bind the texture to unit 0
    glActiveTexture(GL_TEXTURE0);
    glBindTexture(GL_TEXTURE_2D, texture);
```

Delete/Destroy Texture

```
glDeleteTextures(1, &texName);
```

3D Mathematics

Create Projection Matrix

```
glm::mat4 projMat = glm::perspective(glm::radians(viewAngle),
    (float)dispWidth / (float)dispHeight, zNear, zFar);
```

Example values:

- *viewAngle = 60.0f* (so a viewing angle of 60°)

- *dispWidth = 800*

- *dispHeight = 600*

- *zNear = 10.0f*

- *zFar = 10000.0f*

NOTE: The specific values depend on your camera and the scene. For example, the [*zNear*, *zFar*] range depends on the scale of your virtual 3D world.

Translate and Rotate Model/Object

```
glm::mat4 modelMat;
modelMat = glm::translate(glm::mat4(1.0f),
    glm::vec3(posX, posY, posZ));
modelMat = glm::rotate(modelMat, (float)angle, glm::vec3(axisX, axisY,
axisZ));
```

Translate and Rotate the Camera

IMPORTANT: View matrix transformations are the inverse of those done with the model/object. See the section on page 25 for details.

```
glm::mat4 viewMat;

viewMat = glm::translate(viewMat,
```

```
    glm::vec3(-camPosX, -camPosY, -camPosZ));
viewMat = glm::rotate(viewMat, (float)-angle, glm::vec3(axisX, axisY, axisZ));
```

Calculate the Model-View (MV) and Normal Matrices

```
glm::mat4 mvMat = viewMat * modelMat;
glm::mat4 normalMat = glm::inverseTranspose(mvMat);
```

Calculate the Model-View-Projection (MVP) Matrix

NOTE: Uses *mvMat* calculated above.

```
glm::mat4 mvpMat = projMat * mvMat;
```

Useful Resources

I'll be adding resources to the Kea Sigma Delta website from time to time: https://keasigmadelta.com/

Reference Manuals (lookup documentation for functions/features):

- C/C++ Standard Library Reference: http://www.cplusplus.com/reference/

- OpenGL ES 3 Reference: https://www.khronos.org/opengles/sdk/docs/man3/html/index.php

- SDL Manual: https://wiki.libsdl.org/FrontPage

Vector/Matrix Libraries:

- GLM (C++): http://glm.g-truc.net/0.9.8/index.html

- Kazmath (C/C++): https://github.com/Kazade/kazmath

3D Mathematics:

- http://chortle.ccsu.edu/vectorlessons/vectorindex.html

Forums & Websites:

- https://www.opengl.org/discussion_boards/

- https://reddit.com/r/opengl/

- https://www.gamedev.net/

Books:

Books on this topic tend to be rather big, heavy on theory, and intimidating to beginners. I have yet to come up with a short-list of what I think the best books are. Future updates to this book may include a shortlist of books.

Resources to Avoid

There are lots of OpenGL tutorials and examples out there using old deprecated functions. If you see any tutorials containing *glBegin()* and *glEnd()*, then run! That's old OpenGL 1.x stuff.

You should never use them (and they don't exist in OpenGL ES, anyway). The same goes for any tutorials using *glLight()*.

Likewise, tutorials using old version 1 GLSL are best avoided. They have variables declared as *varying* instead of *in* or *out*.

www.ingramcontent.com/pod-product-compliance
Lightning Source LLC
Chambersburg PA
CBHW041431050326
40690CB00002B/509